STRUGGLE BEHIND BARS

A Manual on Interrogation, Steadfastness, and Revolutionary Resistance

Dar Al-Raya Publications

Translated from Arabic

CONTENTS

PREFACE

Revolutionaries love life, and they do not hesitate to risk their lives in order to create a free and dignified existence for their people. A life subject to restrictions, oppression, and exploitation is not truly life — it is a miserable condition that must be changed.

True revolutionaries are the candidates for change. They aim to overturn the existing equations of power. In the midst of their struggle to achieve this, they are exposed to the most horrific forms of torture and oppression as the ruling authorities attempt to break their will, demoralize them, and discourage them from continuing. Yet those who are focused on the future and grounded in the realities of their age persevere undeterred. They are the conquerors of the heavens and the makers of the future.

This booklet examines one of the most critical stations in a revolutionary's journey: the interrogation cell. It is an intense stage in which the conflict between the old and the new — between freedom and slavery, between hope and the enemies of hope, between revolution and counter-revolution — takes its most concentrated form.

In the general context of struggle, revolutionary movements resist the machinery of repression. Their best members stand firm under the most extreme circumstances, giving testimony with a clear conscience, never betraying their comrades. Resilience accumulates and grows in the heritage of revolutionary movements and in the people themselves, brick by brick, through the struggles of fighters — so that every fighter who comes after them is fortified by what those before them endured.

The Palestinian national movement began building this heritage long ago, carving out a path of honor and symbolism. The steadfastness of its fighters has been remarkable in its intensity and extraordinary in its ferocity.

> *"In every human being there is weakness and strength, courage and surrender, purity and deceit. The brave resist; the treacherous betray; the weak succumb to despair; the hero fights."*

PART ONE THE FIGHTER AND THE REVOLUTION

The Four Stations of the Palestinian Fighter

As long as the Palestinian fighter remains in the ranks of the revolution, four stations await him:

1. Martyrdom — and how glorious it is for the fighter to choose martyrdom deliberately, for it is the highest degree of sacrifice. In the last decade and a half, the revolution has offered more than one thousand martyrs on the altar of the national struggle, until it became almost impossible to emerge from one cascade of blood only to find oneself floating in another.

Martyrdom may come in the battles of armed revolution, fought with unparalleled heroism in Jordan and Lebanon, or in resistance operations within the occupied homeland. It may also take the form of political assassination — the intelligence services of the Zionist enemy have a long history of targeting the cadres of the revolution — or it may occur under waves of torture during interrogation. Many Palestinian fighters have been martyred in the enemy's prisons, most of them during interrogation.

2. Deportation — the enemy uses this weapon to expel active members from their homeland. More than six hundred deportees have been expelled. The enemy also encourages those facing pressure to request

deportation voluntarily, in addition to the mass displacements that took place in 1948 and the ongoing annual migration exceeding one thousand persons per year.

3. Exile — the fighter refuses to surrender to enemy forces and resorts to living underground within the homeland to continue the struggle. Due to the geography of Palestine and the strength and modernity of the enemy's forces, some revolutionary groups have been compelled to go underground. The Gaza Strip has had a particularly rich experience with this form of resistance.

4. Arrest — the so-called "shama'a" method, which is the enemy's technique of subjecting the fighter to physical and psychological terror, followed by years of captivity. To date, the Zionist enemy has arrested more than eleven thousand Palestinians, including more than seven thousand who have spent over ten years in captivity.

How Arrest Occurs

Arrest takes various forms. The fighter may be summoned by the police, ambushed by enemy intelligence while carrying out a political or military mission, captured in large-scale battles as happens in Lebanon, or raided at home at night accompanied by military demonstrations of force.

The Balance of Power in Interrogation

The balance of power in the interrogation room tilts in favor of the enemy, as it possesses the instruments of coercion. However, the fighter is not without weapons. He possesses something that cannot be besieged: the moral weapon of his faith, his fighting spirit, his courage, his humanity, and his integrity — all of which clash bitterly with the enemy's material weapons.

The intelligence officer operates from behind his torture machine with the aim of destroying the fighter and draining him completely. He seeks to turn the fighter into nothing — to extract the secrets he holds and crush him, leaving him without will or goals. The officer surrounds him, isolates him, pressures him, and punishes him, believing the fighter will collapse today or tomorrow — broken and decayed, with no fighting spirit or humanity left.

The interrogator suggests to the fighter that the investigation is endless and that no one cares about his fate; that his comrades continue their lives and travels in freedom — and that the only way out of this predicament is to surrender his decision and his will.

But those who believe that collapse saves them from the intelligence services are ignorant of how these services operate. Admitting to danger does not protect you from it. The intelligence services repay any concessions they extract with increased pressure. They celebrate a breakthrough, then double their demands. The fighter who stands firm like a towering rock, unyielding and uncompromising, eventually forces them to retreat.

Victory Through Steadfastness

The Palestinian national movement has produced many examples of fighters who stood firm against the most relentless interrogation. Historical memory is long. Tens of thousands of fighters across the world have demonstrated this possibility. In our Palestinian experience, a long list of names includes those who, like Qasim Abu Akar and Nader Al-Afouri, became permanent symbols of heroism under torture.

The revolutionary fighter who sacrifices his life in struggle possesses the most important element of resistance: the will to persevere, to not give in and not submit. He realizes that what he and his comrades build with their nerves and years of struggle must not be squandered under a bundle of sticks — and that what they protect with their blood at the beginning of an investigation must still be protected at its end.

Cooperation with the enemy during interrogation is a crime. It means betraying the secrets of comrades and the revolution, and causing confusion and mistrust among the ranks of the oppressed and their supporters. If he was a hero before his arrest, the fighter who is ready at the critical moment — ready to do whatever serves the revolution and the cause — will remain a hero.

PART TWO FACTORS DETERMINING THE OUTCOME

It is impossible to list all the factors that influence the outcome of an interrogation, as they are numerous and not always the same. However, examining experience closely reveals the decisive ones:

1. Revolutionary Ideology and Organizational Heritage

Revolutionary ideology means, among other things, cultivating a revolutionary spirit in fighters and providing their initial preparation. The heritage of a faction — its history of struggle and organization, its positions, and the degree of its sophistication and cohesion — is reflected in the minds and conduct of its members. A party with rich heritage and deep roots produces steadfast fighters. A weak, fragmented, and crude faction with no heritage can only produce weak, fragmented, and crude elements unable to face interrogation with maturity and courage.

It is difficult, if not impossible, for the enemy to extract a confession from an experienced fighter who is deeply committed to the revolution and has united with it in an indissoluble bond. For such a fighter, surrendering his soul is easier than surrendering a hidden secret.

2. The Type of Person and Personal Background

The degree of the fighter's political and ideological awareness, his understanding of the difficulty of the path he has chosen and his suitability for it, the pattern of his political upbringing, the validity of his convictions, his level of psychological maturity and life experience, the strength of his character, and his social connections — all of these aspects find expression during interrogation. On this basis, the intelligence officer approaches him, targeting his weaknesses and exploiting them.

3. The Will of the Fighter

The will of the fighter determines his strength and steadfastness. The goal he is fighting for, and the degree of his commitment to it, determines his will. Those with great goals — those who struggle for years, even decades — refine themselves through that struggle. Those who cannot continue fall by the wayside. Only the strongest, most committed, and most sacrificial fighters are able to persevere. The will hardens through the deepening of ideological awareness, relentless struggle, daily work, immersion in the overall cause, and the study of revolutionary experiences around the world.

4. Organizational Technique

The method of construction, the laws governing the organization, its structural arrangement, and the conditions of membership and duties — these have a profound effect on what happens during interrogation.

A faction that lacks experienced leaders — or whose leaders rose to their positions through luck rather than gradual progression — is bound to make fatal mistakes leading to its destruction. A militant organization in which political organization is not clearly separated from military organization, and which allows for significant interference between the two, cannot escape fatal blows. An organization that burdens its members with tasks exceeding their capabilities and qualifications is bound to collapse under the heavy load.

An organization that does not observe the principles of internal and external security cannot conceal its exposed extensions. An organization that reduces itself to a single center will not be able to survive a sustained arrest campaign. An organization plagued by internal chaos and neglect is easier to break on the day of reckoning. A small mistake in normal times can have enormous destructive effects under the conditions faced by factions whose leaders are wanted by the occupier.

5. Class and Social Composition

The class content of a faction is the determining factor behind its political ideology and the ideology of its members — their characteristics and psychological foundations. A bourgeois faction will remain narrow-minded regardless of its ambitions; it cannot attain the level of a workers' party with high-level leadership and practical experience. The working class is the most internally unified and revolutionary social class, and its parties are the most principled and skilled.

This is not an absolute rule. Some non-leftist parties have achieved high levels of unity and cohesion, and some leftist organizations have disintegrated under the weight of oppression. But the historical tendency is clear: the more leftist parties develop their struggles and ideological awareness, and the more they elevate qualified cadres to leadership positions, the stronger and more solid their ranks become.

6. The Conditions of Detention

The conditions under which a fighter is detained have a real impact on the human being. A detainee who is confronted with clear evidence — publications, documents, or the confessions of others — faces a more difficult situation than one detained on mere suspicion. He is called upon to show double resilience to repel the enemy's attack and defeat it.

The enemy's intelligence apparatus has two divisions: the intelligence-gathering branch and the investigation branch. There is a clear distinction between interrogation based on unconfirmed information and interrogation based on confirmed material evidence. In the first case, a little resilience can leave the investigators empty-handed and confused. In the second case, greater denial and rejection is required.

Whether the fighter is experienced or untrained, he can refute evidence against him and exit the predicament with honor. The examples are countless. There are also those who confessed and repented — who, as soon as they realized the full gravity of what they had done, rebelled against their statements and retracted them. Some of them paid a high price for this. But rebellion and the pressure that follows it are better than allowing the collapse to make the fighter easy prey for his enemies and his comrades.

7. Arresting the Person in Charge

The person in charge holds many keys and secrets of the work. This places upon him a special burden. The responsibilities that are an honor from the perspective of the revolution are viewed as dangerous liabilities by the enemy. It is the duty of the official to protect his responsibilities as he would protect the most precious thing he possesses.

His steadfastness inspires his comrades with tremendous moral momentum. The humiliation of mass arrest, and the humiliation of comrades facing each other in the interrogation rooms, are compounded immeasurably when a leader falls. A true leader never falls. Just as he has a positive moral influence on his followers in a state of steadfastness, he has a profoundly negative impact in a state of collapse.

When a leader collapses, the secrets of the struggle — which had been like a deaf fortress — are laid waste. His conscious withdrawal from the cause leaves his enemies delighted and the cause of the revolution damaged.

But his comrades, who respected and modeled themselves after their leader, should not allow themselves to be shaken into abandoning the revolution simply because their leader proved to be false. The scientific position requires adherence to revolutionary principles and rejection of their negative manifestations. Steadfastness and loyalty to the revolution are not contingent on the steadfastness or collapse of individuals; they stem from the inner convictions within each comrade. The revolution's train moves forward regardless.

PART THREE INVESTIGATION AND HUMAN FORMATION

The enemy realizes that human beings are not only physical creatures — they are also their minds and souls. This understanding makes it utterly ruthless in deploying the most degrading methods to destroy the Palestinian human being in his entirety: his mind, his nerves, and his body, with the aim of stripping away his dignity and destroying him as a people.

To facilitate this mission, the enemy requires prior knowledge of its prisoners — their beliefs, their social situation, their habits. It recruits agents and informants to report on those it intends to arrest. It uses physical, psychological, and mental torture. It considers any confession extracted by force to be a victory and an excuse to continue.

When Torture Begins

Contrary to what some believe, torture does not begin during the investigation period. It begins on the first day of occupation and continues thereafter. The enemy wages a complex psychological war against our people and our fighters even before their arrest, and continues this pressure afterward through checkpoints that prevent freedom of movement, military patrols and displays of force, institutional instability and bureaucratic obstruction, the encouragement of bribery and corruption, the fomenting of tribal and sectarian strife, economic and educational pressures, and growing unemployment. All of this serves to sap the vitality of the Palestinian people.

The enemy deliberately hinders citizens' access to government institutions — permits, health services, education, employment — creating a state of collective frustration and humiliation. The accumulation of failure and helplessness, year after year, leads to despair among the masses. This is precisely the purpose of occupation.

To succeed in this psychological war, the enemy relies on the collaboration of Arab employees in public institutions to play the role of petty despots; it relies on a fifth column of agents to spread rumors and persecute those who resist with lies and fear.

The Psychological War Within the Interrogation Room

During the investigation period, the intelligence services surround the detainee with a network of pressure, isolation, loneliness, threats, and terrorism — all working in the same direction and for the same purpose.

The defeat of psychological warfare is achieved through resistance and defiance. Frustration and despair are the paths that lead to hopelessness and internal defeat, and thus to surrender and external collapse. Resistance and defiance lead to self-confidence and resilience, and ultimately to victory.

The enemy has recognized this, and so it forms investigation teams that are designed to counteract this dynamic. It plants harsh interrogators who know no mercy alongside seemingly friendly ones whose role is to absorb the detainee's resentment and prevent it from finding expression in rebellion. The former strike hard; the latter absorb. Both are cut from the same cloth and take turns playing their roles.

Physical and Neurological Methods of Exhaustion

To exhaust the fighter and drain his vitality, the enemy employs methods that are more brutal and cunning: forcing the fighter to run or stand for many days; depriving him of sleep for extended periods; bombarding him with multiple simultaneous questions; shouting and cursing. All of these are means of exhausting the nerves and the brain, causing general physical and psychological collapse.

The nervous system is complex and centered in the brain, which responds and reacts to any external stimuli. It analyzes inputs from all five senses and reacts accordingly — through movement, through hormonal secretions, through changes in blood flow. Continuous disruption of the nervous system exhausts the brain and causes imbalances that make the subject more susceptible to further manipulation.

But the Palestinian fighter is not empty-handed. He is capable of resistance, and his pride and willpower provide him with moral sustenance that the enemy cannot crush. Many fighters have shut their mouths against all of the enemy's methods and fascist theories.

The Lie Detector

One desperate device the enemy uses is the polygraph machine — a device consisting of simple components: a thermometer, a blood pressure gauge, and a respiration monitor. When the detainee is asked normal questions, his baseline readings are recorded. Questions related to the investigation are then inserted, and the deviations are noted.

However, this device is easily foiled. The subject may be afraid of the device itself or of the investigator, or may deliberately imagine disturbing or frightening scenes — all of which confuse the device's readings and render the results meaningless.

The Goal of Cooperation

In the end, the only thing the investigator truly wants is the detainee's cooperation — to create a working relationship between himself and the fighter, in which the fighter responds to orders and gradually opens up. As soon as the fighter refuses his orders and defies them, the investigator's two tools — the harsh interrogator and the friendly one — cease to function. Once the fighter challenges his fear of the investigator even once, he can challenge it many times. The harshest investigation cannot extract what the fighter refuses to give.

The descent from the interrogation chambers to the general prison ward, done with high spirits and a determination to continue as a hammer of justice and perseverance — this is the true measure of victory. And the freedom of the prisoner, bound within prison walls, lies precisely in that — in the celebration of having preserved what he was asked to surrender.

PART FOUR THE THEORY OF INVESTIGATION

The theory of investigation studies the nature of the fierce conflict — fierce in its content, and often fierce in its manifestations — that takes place between representatives of the national movement and investigators in the interrogation chambers.

This conflict is, in essence, a focused expression of the broader struggle between the revolutionary movement — its factions, parties, apparatus, and symbols — and the reactionary, oppressive, fascist occupation and its security apparatus: the judiciary, the police, and the secret police. This broader struggle takes all forms: public and private, legitimate and illegitimate, violent and nonviolent, material and ideological. Its forms are shaped by the militant, psychological, and ideological situation of both parties.

The Antagonistic Nature of the Conflict

The conflict is antagonistic in its essence: the goal of both sides is to completely eliminate the other's capacity for action, whether through tactical or strategic plans or through various means aimed at achieving the inevitable result.

When this conflict is confined to the interrogation room, it takes place between the interrogator — who represents the investigative agencies and employs the methods, tools, categories, and tricks at his disposal — and the detained revolutionary fighter, who responds to the interrogator using every method of resistance at his disposal, defending his cause.

The investigator aims to strip the fighter of his national and class struggle, to destroy his position as a fighter, to break him down. The fighter aims to stand firm, to miss this opportunity for the enemy to prevail, thereby protecting himself, his party, and his national movement from attack.

The Investigator as Employee

The investigator exercises his role as an employee — an employee of the hostile regime that recruited him, prepared him for this role, and demands that he succeed in his mission as a tool and pillar of that regime. The regime provides him with knowledge, mobilizes him, offers him incentives, and grants him the necessary powers to apply various methods of investigation. His goal is to bring the detainee to a state of collapse and complete cooperation, and this goal can only be achieved if the detainee's physical or psychological condition deteriorates completely or partially.

The Fighter as the Opposite Pole

The fighter is the opposite pole: he is the patriot who is determined to fight for freedom; steadfast in his just cause; defending that cause with his physical, psychological, and moral strength, with a degree of firmness appropriate to his situation. His weapon in the interrogation chambers is, first and foremost, his patience and steadfastness — grounded in a preliminary or deep understanding of what happens in interrogation rooms. His weapon is also his dignity, his national pride, and his deep national and ideological affiliation.

As long as the detainee has been thrown into the conflict, the conflict has begun to take its course. It is likely that the strongest ideologically, the strongest in terms of convictions, the deepest in terms of principles, and the most confident will prevail — and the weakest will be eliminated if they fail to persist in resistance.

The fighter wins if he remains in all centers of the investigation, keeping his eyes on the goal of perseverance — knowing the goals he has achieved — and resolving not to betray his comrades, his party organizations, and his national movement, never to betray his people or abandon his cause.

The investigator is, ultimately, an employee performing his routine duties. His power stems from his position and the authorities that surround him. The fighter is someone who believes in a just cause and is not afraid to die for it. The investigation must end — it always ends. And it must end with honor and heroism.

Familiarity as a Weapon

Familiarity with the experience of investigation, its stages of development, and its results — close and distant — provides the fighters and the national movement with a lofty and comprehensive vision. It enriches the fighter with knowledge of what is to come in the investigation, and continues his preparation for martyrdom before arrest, his readiness to sacrifice himself; it continues with him inside the interrogation cells in the light of the theory of resilience and its components.

This aims to enable the detainee to understand the investigation process so that he can remain steadfast, avoid collapse, and avoid falling into traps — while understanding that his resilience will not only be an expression of personal will, but an expression of his revolutionary determination to protect himself as a fighter, to protect his party, his people, and his revolution, thereby supporting and strengthening his cause and keeping the conflict on its ideological course — with awareness and determination — based on loyalty to the revolution and the people.

What Is Resilience?

The detainee is subjected to methods of torture in order to affect him psychologically and physically. Some of these experiences actually occur — he is beaten, he becomes hungry, he works hard for hours and becomes tired, he is deprived of sleep. These symptoms affect the psychological state to varying degrees.

This is the important point: those who are endowed with faith and willpower are affected physically and bodily by the beating — but their spiritual side remains unshaken, because the spiritual aspect does not depend on food and drink but on readiness, especially in moments of struggle.

Resilience means overcoming the physical and moral pressures to which the fighter is exposed. It is completely linked to the root of conviction, which grows, flourishes, and deepens like a living organism, and feeds on previous experience.

The experience of struggle lived in the dungeons of investigation — which is always built on getting through one more hour — is such that an initial steadfastness in the early stages of investigation provides the detainee with a new resolve that adds to the resolve of the previous hours and initial experiences. The steadfastness of the earlier phase nourishes the steadfastness of the subsequent stages. Thus the saying is proved true: "Between victory and defeat lies an hour of patience."

The nutrients of the fighter under investigation are all internal — something as simple as the thought that it would be shameful to confess, that it would be shameful to give information about the house that sheltered him, about his female comrades, about his brothers in struggle — all of this strengthens his steadfastness to the point where all methods of torture and interrogation fail.

Steadfastness as a Personal Trait

Steadfastness, based on the fact that it is a personal trait, enriches the ironclad stance that defies the enemy's will, its tools, and its interrogation methods. It is the art of confronting the enemy everywhere — based on a deep conviction of the justice of the cause and the determination to defend and fight for it. It is evident everywhere and in every circumstance, both inside and outside prison, through direct conflict with the enemy in various battles, including the battle of interrogation.

The revolutionary fighter is steadfast in his principles, steadfast in his convictions, and steadfast in his determination to achieve his goals and defend the just cause from which the revolutionary party whose positions are clear draws its orientations. Here, steadfastness as a commitment to the cause — whatever that cause may be — becomes a quality available to any individual fighter, allowing him to defeat the oppressor and push his methods into bankruptcy.

PART FIVE RESILIENCE AND COLLAPSE

What Is Collapse?

Collapse — or surrender during interrogation — is a state of defeat: a failure that reflects the weakness of the defeated, and a victory for those who prevail through humiliation. It is a state of separation from the challenge; the abandonment of resistance in the face of interrogation, which enables the enemy to obtain the information it wants from the mouth of its opponent, condemn him, and take all punitive measures.

This is a form of treason — conscious or unconscious, it does not ultimately matter — that the detainee commits as a result of his cooperation with the investigator and his disclosure of information and secrets. He betrays his comrades and the party and the revolution, moving from the side of the revolution to the side of its enemies — even if only during the interrogation phase — strengthening the enemies and weakening the revolution from within.

The enemy constantly seeks to infiltrate the revolutionary ranks by recruiting agents. It rarely succeeds in doing so. But in the case of investigation, under the weight of pressure, it seeks to obtain from the detainee a trial of the war and the revolution itself — and sells it through various methods. When it sees that the detainee has been broken, it has for the duration of the investigation recruited one of the elements of the revolution against itself, and carried secrets from within. This is the reality of collapse during investigation.

Common Reasons for Collapse

Many collapses are triggered by what seem, in retrospect, to be trivial matters: being deprived of sleep for a long time; being deprived of cigarettes; having one's honor insulted by the investigator. Others confessed after the investigator swore to them on the Quran or by their religion, and they feared the prohibition on lying before God. Some attributed their confessions to threats of having female relatives assaulted. And the most trivial of all: some gave their testimony after being ordered to remove their clothing.

For these and other reasons, fighters became servants of the intelligence services during the investigation period — and then spent years in the darkness of prisons, followed by the full legal consequences.

Collapse Is a Tragedy

The collapses and confessions are a tragedy for the Palestinian national movement in all their forms and degrees, and they are the strongest weapon used and exploited by the enemy to combat, belittle, and diminish the Palestinian national movement. The unlimited collapses and confessions have resulted in detention centers crowded with thousands of fighters, harsh sentences, and devastating measures against them and those they named.

It is not surprising to find in the camps of the Zionist enemy those who were arrested at one time and completely collapsed — leading to the fall not only of themselves but of entire cells. A single arrest and its collapse can destroy cells of ten or more in one sweep.

Avoiding Collapse

Avoiding collapse is possible and within reach, as demonstrated by hundreds — even thousands — of mature experiences among those who have struggled and kept their information in their hearts despite the severity of the torture. This means they were able to refrain from giving away information, as they themselves confirmed after reviewing the evidence. There are also those who gave false statements during the investigation — statements that had no basis in reality — and the investigation ended without them admitting to the actual charges brought against them.

Once again, the experiences of those who had collapsed confirmed their ability — and the ability of others — to stand firm, after reviewing themselves and realizing that their weakness was not justified, and that all the subjective factors that prompted them to confess during the investigation were worthless. They were able to stand firm; some of them withdrew their confessions and denied their statements after it became clear to them that their confessions had caused terrible damage to themselves and to the revolution.

The Possibility of Recovery

There is also another type of fighter who confessed and repented — who, as soon as they realized the gravity of what they had done, rebelled against their testimony and retracted it. Some of them suffered greatly for this. But the best response when a detainee who has confessed tries to repair the damage is to refuse to cooperate with the evidence he provided against fellow fighters, to rebuke him, and to refuse to work with him even if he begs and cries. This will weaken the investigators' case and may cause the one who collapsed to return to his principles. Rebellion after collapse — and the pressure that follows it — is better than making the collapsed fighter easy prey for his enemies and his comrades.

The Structural and Organizational Causes of Collapse

Responsibility for collapse does not rest solely with the individual fighter. Organizational factors play a decisive role.

First: the degree of membership and preparation. The affiliation of members cannot be separated from their preparation and education. The validity of the militant stance cannot be separated from deepening the fighter's faith and organically linking him to the struggle in its various forms. The high prestige of the organization in the eyes of its fighters strengthens their attachment to it — making it more difficult for the interrogator to cause a rift between the fighter and his organization during interrogation.

Second: educating fighters on all aspects of the investigation process, explaining it in detail and depth, clarifying the fighter's rights during the various stages of investigation — and repeating this explanation, while mobilizing solid and verified examples of those who fought and prevailed, as inspiring evidence of the reality of the cause. This education reduces collapses, so that those who surrender become exceptional cases and resilience becomes the rule.

Third: the formulation and structure of organizations in the right way; preparing activists politically and ideologically; training them in all forms of struggle in accordance with their individual characteristics and level of development; and informing them of all the methods used by the enemy to pursue revolutionaries in various fields and situations, including conditions of necessity. This arms the member with the immediate revolutionary competence that will make him a strong revolutionary fighter in front of the interrogators.

The Illusion That Confession Is Inevitable

During the investigation, the enemy spreads a series of rumors — through the investigator's hands and words — that resistance is impossible; that everyone here admits; that the detainee will not differ from his predecessors, who put everything they had on the table, gently or by force. Speak well and rest easy. This creates an illusion, reinforced by the examples of those who have already collapsed.

The investigator attempts to create a false justification in front of the activist, placing him in a position of: "As long as everyone else is talking, I will talk too" — linking the revolutionary not to revolutionary models but to degenerate models.

Freeing the fighters from the illusion that confession is inevitable is one of the most powerful tools against collapse. This false illusion enables the interrogators to weaken the resolve of even the least experienced fighters. Adding an ironclad confirmation of the falsity of this illusion — through education, through the presentation of real examples — will enable the simplest and least experienced fighter to resist the interrogators and prevail over them.

PART SIX INVESTIGATION METHODS

Based on everything reviewed above, we can conclude that the various investigation methods depend on the type of activist, their position, their degree of steadfastness and awareness, and their location in the conflict. They also depend on whether the activist is considered important in the eyes of the investigators — someone who is tough, loud-mouthed, arrogant, and aware of his position — or whether he is viewed as weak and subjective. In general, the methods of investigation and their application depend on the type of detainee who falls into the investigators' hands, as well as on the type of investigators themselves and their professional personalities.

Two Types of Detainee

The Accidental Detainee

The accidental detainee is someone detained because of some connection to the national movement — motivated by simple nationalist sentiment and acting without having received preparation or education, or because he belongs to one of the organizations without having been politically educated. He has not been transformed into a professional activist who was aware of what he was doing, believed in it, and developed his own national consciousness.

The accidental detainee includes those who, driven by genuine national enthusiasm, participated in some form of resistance without having a comprehensive understanding of the consequences of their actions. It includes those who were arrested because they were relatives of activists, or because they crossed someone's land, or were close to a fighter who was wanted.

The investigator may not find it very difficult to deal with this type of detainee. The methods of deception used against nationalist activists are often effective precisely because the activists have not been adequately prepared and trained in the spirit of heroic steadfastness during interrogation. Many detainees received the education of a backward society — an ideology inherited from feudalism and infused with a selfish bourgeois spirit.

The Professional Detainee

The professional detainee is a citizen who belongs intellectually, politically, and organizationally; who has tied his fate definitively to the wheel of struggle through his party or organization and integrated himself into it completely. His affiliation imbues him with a revolutionary spirit of struggle and increases his willingness to sacrifice. His level of awareness and maturity rises, and he realizes that his actions and struggles are only possible within the organizational reality — that his personal destiny cannot be changed by circumstances; his destiny is determined by his loyalty to the party or organization.

The professional detainee knows what he is doing and understands that his struggles are binding on him — just as he understands that they are a factor in achieving the goals of the party, the class he represents, and the people he serves. He is intellectually and ideologically saturated, and thus represents a powerful pole in front of the investigators. The depth of his commitment and ideology will make him victorious in the struggle if he remains steadfast — his knowledge of the methods of investigation and his readiness for them, despite their severity and harshness.

He realizes that during the investigation, he is engaged in a fierce struggle between what he represents as a political trend and what the interrogator represents as another political direction. He will inevitably prevail — because victory truly belongs to the ideologically righteous, regardless of the material structure of the conflict.

Hundreds, even thousands, of experiences in Palestine and in all countries confirm that professional fighters who are thoroughly prepared are completely immune to the tricks and traps of the enemy. They simply put the investigator in a difficult position. Often, the investigator discovers the solid fact that confronts him, and resorts immediately to torture — not knowing where to start or how to proceed — because the usual methods of simplifying the case, questioning the revolutionary situation, and offering temptations are of no use here.

Method One: The Psychological Approach

The psychological method is a series of structured and programmed practices aimed at influencing the psychological state of the detainee — subjugating him, weakening him psychologically and morally, causing him to lose his inner cohesion, and creating a general imbalance in his psychological state and internal connections, so that he becomes more responsive to certain stimuli and specific reactions.

The psychological state is affected both by the physical condition of the body and by external factors: conversations, stories, and news — whether good or disturbing; ideas that are confirmed or refuted; exaggeration or downplaying; forced positions for the body such as being tied up, suspended, or lying naked.

Casting Doubt and Shaking Connections

This is a set of practices, manifestations, and interpretations aimed at isolating the detainee from his political connections — his organizational and intellectual ties — and treating him as an isolated individual. It addresses his personal capacities for resilience and steadfastness, discouraging him from continuing to deny. It attacks his beliefs and principles with ridicule and contempt. It belittles his ideological beliefs and his practices against the occupation. It portrays him as weak and wrong in his convictions.

The investigator will portray himself as knowing everything, being capable of everything, understanding the political situation deeply and correctly — while the fighter understands it superficially or incorrectly. He will claim that the fighter did not think carefully about the consequences of his actions; that his comrades have all already confessed and been relieved; that only the fighter himself — the stubborn one — remains to suffer.

The investigator also tries to convince the detainee that his comrades were the ones who informed on him, that the party is corrupt, that his leaders are enjoying themselves in comfort while he suffers. All of these are lies. A firm stance is the best way to defeat the method of doubt — regardless of the severity of the conditions the investigator tries to create, and no matter what loopholes he seeks to exploit.

Method Two: Terrorism

Terrorism is the use of brutal material, psychological, and verbal acts — repeated and escalating — intended to inflict physical harm and intimidation. The investigator uses beatings, court appearances, threatening gestures, and tools of torture — all of this to intimidate the activist and shake his morale and connections. The investigator is not aiming to physically exterminate through rounds of torture. He aims to terrorize; to intimidate — in order to achieve the result of confession.

When does the detainee reach the state of collapse under terrorism? Simply — if he is afraid of the procedures. But if the detainee notices that all of these methods have not scared him, the investigator will abandon them. The fighter who is conscious in terms of struggle and knowledgeable about interrogation methods will face this method with one of two possibilities: either the terrorism will lead to a greater fear of confession, so that the detainee fears confession more than he fears torture — and as long as he continues to receive abuse, he will not say anything; or the terrorism will lead to a desperate capitulation.

Professional fighters with a clear revolutionary consciousness face terrorism with unwavering determination. The more oppressive the methods become, the more determined they are to resist. They exhaust the interrogators — all of them, with all their chains and instruments — and defeat them. This is not an exception. It is the rule when fighters are properly prepared.

The Investigator's Limitations

It is important to understand what the investigator cannot do. He can inflict pain. He can expose the hunger striker to fainting. He can exhaust the fighter and cause physical breakdown. He can break a hand. He can continue beating until the fighter faints. But he cannot move the fighter's tongue to reveal secrets without receiving direct cooperation from the fighter himself. He cannot, by these methods alone, take away from the fighter his belief in his cause or his determination to defend it.

Providing information to the investigator is a voluntary act, even if that act occurs under harsh coercive circumstances. The investigator creates these conditions in the torture chambers for all visitors to the chambers — both activists and non-activists, the important and the unimportant. No matter how much the investigator tries to make confession seem expected and natural, it is always a decision made by the fighter himself.

In Summary

The investigation is a process of conflict between two poles: the interrogator, who uses all available methods to force the accused to reveal information about himself, his party, and the movement; and the accused — the militant, whether experienced or untrained — who is subjected to torture and interrogation methods and resists them, seeking to confuse and disrupt them, playing an influential role in the investigation process in order to bring it to a successful conclusion.

The interrogator resorts to futile practices, reaching a state of despair regarding the possibility of obtaining any information. His plan is modified again and again — by the responses, resilience, mood, and disposition of the fighter — until at last, faced with a fighter who remains firm, he announces his defeat to his superiors, though he tries to cover it up.

The investigation must end. It always ends. And it must end with the fighter descending from the upper floors to the prison wards with high spirits and determination — as the hammer of justice and perseverance — having preserved what was asked of him. That is the beginning of freedom.

— End —

Palestinian Political Prisoners

STRUGGLE BEHIND IRON BARS

Published by:

PLO UNIFIED INFORMATION

FOREIGN INFORMATION DEPARTMENT

P.O.B: 145168 Beirut — Lebanon

in cooperation with the

COMMITTEE FOR THE DEFENSE OF POLITICAL PRISONERS IN ISRAELI JAILS

July 1979

CONTENTS

INTRODUCTION

The torture of Palestinian detainees in Zionist jails has become clear and undeniable. The London Sunday Times "Insight" Report on July 19, 1977 and the two secret cables dated May 31 and November 30, 1978 sent by Alexandra Johnson from the U.S. Consulate in Jerusalem to the State Department and published in the Washington Post on February 7, 1979, are but a few examples of reports detailing this torture.

On March 14, 1979, 76 Palestinian political prisoners were liberated from this suffering in Zionist jails and received with open arms by the Palestinian people in the occupied homeland and outside. The incident itself is a significant turning point in the Palestinian-Zionist struggle, the core of the Middle East conflict.

Most important, however, is the strong, persistent and determined will that these militants kept glowing in their hearts through their long years of imprisonment. The occupiers failed to suppress this will in spite of their brutal and inhuman practices. Palestinian prisoners turned their solitary cells into extended bases of the revolution and transformed their pain and suffering into a daily challenge and defiance to their jailers.

In the following pages, some of these liberated militants will tell their own story of their imprisonment behind the iron bars of the Zionist jails.

PLO UNIFIED INFORMATION FOREIGN INFORMATION DEPARTMENT

HASSAN AL-SAGHIR

Born: 1939 | Arrested: 1969

I was arrested on 31 December 1969 in the Galilee area in 1948-occupied Palestine. On my way back to my base, I found myself surrounded by enemy soldiers. I clashed with them for half an hour after which I succeeded in breaking my way out of the siege. I hid among the trees till darkness, then I continued on my way. But then I fell from a high rock and broke my leg. I had no choice but to creep under the trees, not knowing which way to go. My leg swelled severely. For two days I didn't have any water or food. I was very tired, so I went to sleep. I woke up to find five enemy soldiers surrounding me, one of them pushing the barrel of his gun against the back of my head. After beating me severely, they blindfolded me, tied my hands and dragged me some distance until I was thrown into a jeep. I was taken to Acre prison.

TORTURE

The interrogation lasted for more than two months. I don't think that any of us went through the interrogation without becoming ill or disabled. I myself almost lost my hearing in one of my ears, and now suffer from rheumatism.

They extinguished cigarettes on my skin. The nails of my fingers and toes were brutally pulled out. They put my hands on the edge of a table and started beating me on the nails till they swelled up and bled. Then they pulled the nails with pincers.

I was asked many times to hold up a heavy object and keep standing for several hours. Whenever I tried to put my hands down, they started beating me. After I broke down they beat me and demanded that I hold it up again. For several days I was left without food or water. They would tie my hands with a rope and hang me from a tree. I was left that way for several hours till my wrists bled. After that they put me into a sack and threw me in front of police dogs that would attack and bite me. When they let me have a rest, they tied my hands and legs and threw me into a small narrow cell, the floor of which was filled with water. I could neither sit nor sleep.

All these tortures were inflicted because I refused to give the names of the group I went into occupied Palestine with, or the names of people we met there. I refused as well to show them on the map the base I came from.

THE TRIAL

During the trial I was charged with belonging to an "illegal" organisation, i.e. the PLO, crossing the "Israeli" border without a permit, belonging to an armed group, organizing groups inside "Israel", and clashing with the Israeli forces. The judge asked me to admit my guilt, but I refused and told them: "My organisation, the PLO, is a legal one and represents the struggle and aspirations of my people whom you drove out of their land. Its legality is recognized by all the forces of peace and justice in the world. It is my duty and right to return to my land which you drove me out of. Nothing will bar my way back and I will never recognize your entity nor ask for your permission to return. It is my duty to struggle against you for the sake of my people and cause."

After three sessions of the trial, I refused to admit guilt and didn't recognize their law. I said to the judge: "You say that I entered in an illegal way. But I want to ask you yourself, from where did you come to my land, and how? Maybe you came from America, Europe or Africa. Maybe you even came from an Arab country. Did you come here in a legal way? You, who infiltrated into my country and usurped my land and home, are trying me, the owner of the land and the home. What an irony!"

The judge got angry and shouted: "Shut up!" Some policemen started beating me. After that I was given a life sentence. There were reporters attending the trial. When a pressman noticed me laughing, he came towards me asking: "You have received a life sentence, but you are laughing." I said: "It's a medal of honour to decorate my militant march."

RAMLE PRISON

After that I was taken by two policemen to a military car. The car drove to the Ramle prison. I was put in a special wing called "Argav". There I met my fellow militants and began adapting my life to the conditions in the prison.

The Ramle prison is a central one with access for visitors from abroad. This makes the treatment in this prison relatively better than in other prisons, for propaganda purposes. Prisoners were supplied with books: books of history, religion and political books. History books are totally forged, especially those that deal with the Arab-Zionist conflict. They distort the justice of our cause and the rights of our people; they give all the right to the Jewish people as being "chosen by God". The land is "theirs", and they have the "right" to live on it.

STRUGGLE

Late in 1970, our fellow prisoners in Ashkelon prison declared a hunger strike in protest against living conditions in the prison. A meal was not sufficient even for a five-year-old child. They were badly treated: daily beaten, tortured and lashed. Even their relatives, whenever they came to visit them, were beaten and insulted. Health conditions were deteriorating. So we declared a hunger strike in Ramle prison in solidarity with our fellow prisoners in Ashkelon.

The prison chief, Ilias, asked us: "What have you got to do with those in Ashkelon? You have your own conditions and they have theirs. Everything is going well."

Our answer was simply that: "We are members of the same revolution. Everywhere in your prisons, we consider ourselves united. It is our duty to confront you, so that our fellow prisoners may have human living conditions." His reaction was: "If you go on strike, I will transfer you to your fellows in Ashkelon." And so he did. I was one of the group transferred.

ASHKELON

All the prisoners were participating in the hunger strike. Even those with bad health insisted on taking part. Abdel Kader Abu Al-Fahm, former leader of the popular liberation forces in Gaza in 1968, died while carrying out the strike. He was very ill but refused to end his hunger strike, saying: "I am one of you, and I will continue with you." Another militant, Khalil from Khan Younis, suffered health breakdown and had to have his leg amputated.

The strike in a prison is the most effective weapon you have against your enemy. The reaction of the prison authorities was to force-feed those who passed out and lost consciousness, using a plastic pipe through the mouth into the abdomen. This caused an ulcer in many cases. This was meant to destroy the strikers physically and psychologically in a slow way.

IN BEIT LEED PRISON

In 1972, I was transferred with others to Beit Leed prison. There, we found the same suffering and bitter conditions. We had to struggle to have our social conditions improved, to have better treatment and living conditions.

We started to organize ourselves and to be alert for agents the enemy was trying to plant among us.

Moreover, we began to prepare cultural programs and to mobilize ourselves against the Zionist propaganda.

Later that year, the situation in the prison worsened and our relations with the prison authorities deteriorated. As usual, we had our own leadership in the prison and a reserve one in case the acting one was moved to another prison. After that we declared a Strike.

On the seventh day of the strike, the general director of the prison, Neir, and the minister of police, Shlomo Helil, came to question us. We gave them our demands. They said that they would answer all our demands if we ended the strike. But our experience with their promises and words of "honour" convinced us to refuse to end the strike unless our demands were met first. Their reaction was to use the most oppressive measures against us. At the beginning of 1973, they transferred some of us to Beersheba prison under the pretext of our being leaders of the strike. I was one of those transferred.

IN BEERSHEBA PRISON

Our living conditions and treatment were no better. The organizational matters were wretched. There were some privileges for those who agreed to work in the workshops related to the prison. Of course these privileges arose from the fact that these prisoners were strengthening the Zionist economy and providing additional manpower to the enemy. They made clothes, towels and carpets for the Zionist soldiers and camouflage nets for their tanks. So we began to organize them, rebuild their spirit and teach them that any work that benefits the enemy is treason against our cause and people.

NO WORK FOR THE ZIONIST WAR ECONOMY

"This was not an easy task for us. It took us several months until our efforts were fruitful. After that we declared a strike. We called for better treatment, better meals — both in quantity and quality — and an end to work in the workshops. That was the period of the October war. We told our fellow prisoners that it was treason to work in the Zionist workshops and replace the Zionist workers who went to the front to fight our people and nation. We said this to the prison director, Berzlai: 'We came to destroy you, not to work for you. If we were to do any work in the prison, it would be for our own and our brothers' benefit, but not yours. We work in the kitchen, wash our clothes, assist our sick comrades, but we will not work in your factories and workshops.'

"He offered us an improvement in our conditions, an increase in the quantity of food for our meals, and a longer visiting period, all on the condition that we end the strike and resume work in the workshops. We rejected the offer saying that the issue of work is the corner stone of our struggle inside the prison."

EDUCATION

"Some of our fellow prisoners were uneducated or even illiterate. But some of us were teachers or able to teach. The Red Cross supplied us with the books we needed on educational, historical, philosophical, political and religious subjects. We supplied our library with about 500 books. We had our own programs for education and general knowledge. We held lectures on different subjects. We studied the Arab-Israeli conflict: how and when did it start. How to deal with it. Of course, these books were written from the Zionist point of view, but we had our own evaluation and analysis. Within four years, we rebuilt the political personality of our fellow militants in the prison, after a period of hopelessness.

"It is true that we suffered very much in the prisons. But we were able to transform the sufferings and pains into a revolutionary knowledge which strengthened our belief in our revolution and cause. We used to prepare our own studies concerning certain incidents and to come out with a comprehensive scientific analysis about them."

SOURCES OF INFORMATION

"Our sources of information were the Israeli radio and press, and from time to time other foreign newspapers. Of course, the news that the Israeli radio and press conveyed was totally forged, but our experience made us capable of reading between the lines. For example, when the news said that a fire broke out or an explosion erupted in a factory, we guessed that there was a commando operation behind it."

"Some of us in Beersheba prison knew English, and others knew Hebrew. We had an administrative committee, an organizational committee, an interrogation committee and a cultural committee. Each ran its own affairs. The cultural committee, for example, was responsible for preparing a report under the title: 'Know Your Enemy'."

"However, the prison authorities did not approve of our organizational, cultural and educational activities. They considered these activities, though we were within the prison, as violating their security. Haiem Halivi, the director of the prisons, sent an investigative team to the prison, but we refused to meet them. He then came with a police squad who rushed into our rooms and began inspections. They began beating us and rounded up about 90 of us. Halivi began shouting and screaming at us saying: 'What does this mean? Are you establishing your own authority in the prison? There will be no authority inside the prisons except mine!'"

"They took us then to Toulkarm prison. After that I was transferred to Jenin prison. I stayed there till my release."

ABDEL RAHIM JABER

Born: 1938 | Arrested: 1968

I was arrested in very difficult conditions. My arrest was after the "Night of Bombs" in Jerusalem and the explosion in the central station in Tel Aviv. I knew that I was being pursued by the Israeli soldiers. I kept out of sight till I met with them face to face in Wadi-Araba. A fierce battle took place between a comrade of mine and myself on one hand and the Israeli soldiers on the other. My comrade was killed and I received 16 wounds all over my body and head, so I could resist no more. This was on 21 September 1968. On my arrest, I was severely beaten before receiving any first aid. Then I was carried to a nearby landing helicopter. Meanwhile, I was bleeding badly. My legs were tied by a rope to the bottom of the helicopter, which took off leaving me hanging in space. I lost consciousness and woke up later in Beersheba hospital. I received some first aid, but the Israeli secret service refused to let me remain hospitalized, and insisted on taking me to Sarafand prison.

There, I was in very wretched health. For four days before the clash with the Zionist soldiers, I had been walking without having any food or water. As a result of hunger, thirst and loss of blood, my eye sight became so weak that I couldn't find my way.

Yet they prevented me from sleeping, insisting that I give them the information they wanted.

The next day Aharon Yariv, minister of police, came and said, "We are not going to let you sleep. I give you ten minutes to speak or I'll know what to do with you then." After ten minutes he brought an electric instrument connected to wires which he fastened to my ears. It gave electric shocks which violently shook my entire body. I felt great pain and shouted involuntarily. This process was repeated for several days.

When it failed to make me confess, they used another kind of torture. They put a thin straw-like instrument into my penis so violently that it bled after they pulled the instrument out. This was in addition to extinguishing cigarettes on my body, especially in my wounds. The deliberate exploitation of my wounds hurt me so much that I lost consciousness many times. This occurred eight times in 52 days, after which they would take me to Hadassa hospital. In addition to this physical torture, they used to carry me and move around to other cells to make me see other militants being tortured and beaten while hanging upside down from the roof. This was a psychological torture meant to make me confess.

On the 25th day of my arrest, I suffered from gangrene in my broken leg and bugs began to creep from beneath the bandage on it. They took me back to Hadassa hospital where they put me in the yard. People crowded around me and began beating and torturing me to the satisfaction of the policemen there, who passively stood by smiling. But when my life became endangered, they took me in a Land Rover to a helicopter which took off and landed on the roof of the hospital. I was hospitalized in the maternity section, which I thought would be safe for me. But after they had supplied me with a glucose unit, some women came and began beating me while some of them tried to cut the pipes of the glucose unit and others attempted to make a hole in it and add water to it. I began to shout till a doctor came and shooed them away.

After that I was taken to Ramle prison where I was kept alone in a separate cell. The treatment there was very bad. For ten months I wasn't allowed to be visited by relatives or to have any contacts with them.

After that I was taken for trial in Hebron prison.

TRIAL

I was charged on 11 counts. It is true that I had clashed with them, but I was charged with being the leader of the forces in the occupied territories. During the trial, the judge read the charges and called me to admit them, saying: "Be a man and confess." My response was "I don't suspect my courage and manhood, but I am totally skeptical of you and your legitimacy. What right do you have to try me on my land?" He added, "You are an infiltrator into other people's land and your rifle is not licensed." I said, "The land is mine and I have the right to come and live on it."

Eventually, I was given five life sentences plus 54 years. After the sentencing, I was taken to Ashkelon prison where I stayed till I was liberated.

ASHKELON PRISON

In Ashkelon, I was held for 40 days in solitary confinement after which I was taken to the director of the prison, who warned me against any activity or provocation. He warned that otherwise I would be subjected to "more beating and torture." After that I was taken to a room where I met other militants. It was the first time I had met another Palestinian or Arab for about eleven months. The militants there formed a very tight unity. They noticed my poor health and received me in a very revolutionary and militant manner. They saved me a special place which they covered with a mattress. They did all they could to make me feel comfortable. They made a decision to give me all their daily shares of meat and eggs to help my health improve and my wounds recover. Though each prisoner's share of meat was only about 30 grams daily, I was able to eat the portions of about 20 persons, and it was a sufficient meal.

In two months, I had recovered and my health was good. When I became able to walk again and go out during the daily half an hour break, I found the conditions difficult and the treatment unbearable. Prisoners have to walk in twos. They mustn't talk or turn their heads right or left. The regulations were oppressive. A patient may suffer without anybody being allowed to treat him. It is true that there was a "pharmacy" in the prison, but the medicine the pharmacist gave for all kinds of ailments was aspirin: If you had an ulcer, he gave you an aspirin. If you had rheumatism, he gave you an aspirin. Nothing but this "magic" aspirin.

"PAPA... PAPA..."

I was prevented from receiving letters from, or sending any to, my family. All that they gave me was a part of the letter with only the words, "Dear father,..." When I was arrested I left a pregnant wife and five young daughters. My wife gave birth to a new daughter whom I didn't see till she was in the third elementary class (about eight years old). The first time my children visited me I couldn't recognize them. Once, during the visiting period, I stood behind the iron barred window seeing how other prisoners were happily talking to their closest relatives. I saw some children running behind the bars. Then they came peeping through the bars as if looking for somebody. I asked them who they were looking for. "We are looking for our father," they said. "But what is your father's name?" I asked. I was shocked to hear them say "Abdel Rahim Jaber!" Believe me tears fell from my eyes as I said, "I am Abdel Rahim Jaber. I am your father!" The children were surprised and bewildered, not believing what they had heard. Then my father came and told them, "This is your father." They put their fingers through the iron bars and I kissed them. I couldn't help shedding tears of sorrow when they began to shout: "Papa, come out. We want to kiss you."

STRUGGLE

We were aware that we were in the enemy's hands and we had to shoulder our responsibilities. We began to organize our ranks and decided on certain measures to confront the problems facing us.

We declared a hunger strike and formed a committee to deal with the strike and strikers' affairs. The committee handed the prison authorities a list of our demands which included intellectual, health, treatment and nutrition demands. We demanded books and reading and study facilities; we demanded treatment for those who were sick and surgery for those needing it. They ignored us for some 4 or 5 days. Then they began to interrogate us separately. When we persisted in the strike, they force-fed us through plastic tubes stuck through the mouth to the stomach.

The authorities pretended to agree to our demands. But one month later, when we realized that we had been deceived, we resumed the hunger strike. Though some demands were met, the necessary things were delayed.

ANOTHER STRIKE

In 1973, we declared another strike. We refused to receive visitors, to accept medicine from the prison authorities, to go out during the breaks and to shave or bathe. The authorities remained passive for about a month. Then they started arguing with us. During the argument the director pushed a blind prisoner, Mahmoud Abu Danhash, violently onto the floor. The director's violence towards our blind comrade provoked a reprisal from us. We attacked the director and his assistant, causing a big unit of the police to come in and attack us with gas and rifle butts. About 100 of us were hurt. Some received head wounds and had their limbs broken. We were driven to the cells and deprived of our belongings and beds.

However, we didn't expect our enemy to be generous or humane to us. By 1976, we had matured and resorted to a hunger strike once again. After the first ten days, some of us broke down, mainly those who were ill. The authorities resorted to the old tactic of force feeding the strikers. I lost two teeth while they were forcing open my mouth with the wooden pincers. Others vomited blood after pulling the plastic pipe out of their stomachs. The strike lasted for 45 consecutive days. After that, Haiem Halivi, general director of the prisons, and Jesterfield, director of our prison, came to talk to us. The committee met them and presented to them our demands. We wanted to be considered prisoners of war and we wanted a redress of our previously mentioned grievances. They promised to meet our demands. The strike was resumed a month later when we realized that we had been deceived. The new strike lasted for 22 days. Though on the material level the strikes did not achieve very much, there were moral and political gains. Moreover, through the strike, we tested our will, which proved to be stronger than our oppressors.

A MATTER OF PRINCIPLE

I want to point out that most of us were offered short sentences if we submitted a plea for mercy. Even those with very long terms were to benefit from this. All of us refused the offer. Why? Because to plea to our enemy for mercy would have been a betrayal of our national principles and humiliating besides. We had consciously and deliberately chosen the path of revolution. Revolution is not a picnic.

ARAB PALESTINE TO LIVE

The news of our release was received as happily by our comrades staying behind as by us. When we bade them farewell, their eyes shed the tears of sincere happiness. In spite of the beatings they would suffer, they shouted to us as we left: "Down with Israel. Long live Arab Palestine!"

MAHMOUD ABU DANHASH

Born: 1948 | Arrested: 1969

I was arrested after being injured in a battle with enemy soldiers in Halhoul area. I was hunted till I was surrounded by the enemy on all sides. There was a battalion of them. I decided to fight to the last and there the battle began. My place was fortified with rocks. The battle continued for a considerable time, until my hand grenades ran out and I was left with a few bullets. I stopped shooting. The soldiers thought I had been killed, but nevertheless a group of them drew near, telling me, through a loudspeaker, to surrender, just in case I was still alive. But no sooner had they come within range, than I reopened fire. The shooting resumed till I had completely run out of ammunition. At that moment, I noticed the serious wounds I had received, the worst of which was a shrapnel in the right eye, which became blind. When I found I had nothing left to fight with, I destroyed my rifle by striking it on the rocks, so the enemy would not benefit from it.

I stayed where I was until they came and seized me. From the moment, the beatings started, with fists, legs and rifle butts. An enemy officer took his pistol and hit me on the upper part of my left eye socket. The bone was broken and I eventually lost sight in my left eye as well. The result of the battle was that I had received about 25 injuries, but the enemy also suffered casualties, including Dogh, the leader of the group, who was killed in the battle.

DETAINED

I was taken to Hebron prison where I was left for several days without receiving any serious medical treatment. This was their response to my refusal to give them information about the other commandos I was in action with. The interrogator asked me, "Why did you come here?" My answer was, "I came to fight and destroy your illegal entity and liberate my land." To that he slapped me on the face. Of course, being blind, I could not anticipate the blow.

TRIAL

I was taken back to Hebron prison for my trial. The trial was superficial. They say that they appoint an attorney to defend the person arrested, but he is usually a secret police officer whose duty is to extract more information from the prisoner to make his situation worse. I refused the attorney they appointed, and demanded the right to appoint an attorney who would really defend me. When they refused I said that I could defend myself.

At another session of the trial, the judge prevented me from expressing myself concerning their illegal entity and our right to live on our land. The police guard hit me on the nose where the bone was already broken. This was in compliance with the judge's orders, and was done in presence of a representative of the International Red Cross. Then I told the court,

"Why are you trying me then, if you aren't going to let me express myself? Give me the sentence you want."

IN ASHKELON PRISON

I spent seven years there. The conditions were very bad. The treatment was very humiliating. Yet, they wanted us to work in the prison workshops and be productive. They fiercely punished those who refused to work.

HUNGER STRIKE

So we declared a hunger strike on 11 December 1976. Our demands were that wounded and disabled prisoners be released. I was one of those named to be released. Another disabled prisoner had his legs amputated. A third one was suffering from a severe fever due to which he was almost mentally disturbed. Other demands were the improvement of the conditions and treatment in the prison, and that the murderers of Omar Shalabi be tried.

The hunger strike lasted for 45 days. On the 9th day, some of us broke down when the authorities managed to force-feed us with a cup of milk by means of a plastic pipe drawn through the nose to the stomach. On the 20th day, they moved some prisoners to other prisons, thinking that they were the leaders of the strike and that upon their departure everything would go back to normal. On the 30th day they moved another group. Yet, in spite of this, all the strikers, even those moved to other prisons, continued the hunger strike, which finally ended on 24 January 1977 on the committee's orders.

RELEASE

When I was released I was in Beersheba prison. A jailer came and called my name and that of three others in the room. He told us to go to the store room of the prison to take our belongings and return the clothes we were wearing, for they were prison property. We were taken in a car belonging to the military police. At the gate of the prison we were transferred to a bus. This was also strange, for the first time since our imprisonment we were riding a bus. Our hands and legs were tied. On the way we heard the soldiers in the bus talking about beating us, but an officer told them not to do so because the International Red Cross was going to check us.

KHALID ABDEL RAHIM ALI

Born: 1945 | Arrested: 1967

After the June war of 1967, I was sent with other militants on a reconnaissance and training mission in the West Bank. We travelled several times between Jordan and the West Bank, taking advantage of the travel policy of the occupation authorities which aimed at emptying the occupied territories of their population. On 18 December, we were arrested while we were on our way to Jordan.

TORTURE

I was taken to Sarafand prison which I can call a torture compound. For 22 days, I was put in a 125 x 75 cms. cell in which I had my meals, slept and which I was forced to use as a toilet. They took me each day to a room and hung me up on its roof with my hands and legs chained. I was beaten with sticks, lashes and rubber pipes continuously for four hours. This was only interrupted by pouring hot and cold water on me whenever I got faint.

At night they would fire guns outside my cell and play sounds of people crying and sighing so that I thought they had shot somebody. They threatened to let police dogs attack me. In fact, they let one of those dogs in my cell and left it the whole night there, so I couldn't sleep.

TRIAL

Six months following my arrest, I was taken to court in Toulkarm. I was charged with being an "infiltrator", joining an "illegal" organisation, "illegal" possession of arms and carrying out military operations.

In reality, I was not arrested in a direct battle with their forces. The charge of "military operations" is directed against any arrested militant. Explosions and military operations in which they fail to detect those responsible would be attributed to any newly arrested militant. At the end of the trial, I was sentenced to 40 years imprisonment. After the trial, I was taken to Ramle prison. I spent a few months there after which I was transferred to Beit Leed prison. At the end I was settled in Ashkelon prison. This was on 10 February 1969.

ASHKELON PRISON

This prison was built by the Zionist authorities to contain the militants coming from outside the occupied territories. The procedure followed there is that each new resident would be put in a solitary cell for 15 continuous days. In the meantime, he would be beaten three times a day, once before each meal. After this "reception" he would be taken to join the other militants in the prison.

HUMILIATION

The treatment I found in Ashkelon prison was no better than that I met during the interrogation period.

We were forced to have our caps and shoes on for 16 hours a day. We had to keep sitting on the floor with our legs bent under us and our blankets strapped in front of us, not allowed to use them till 9:00 P.M. These four blankets, worn out and of bad quality, were to be used as a mattress, a cover and a cushion. Our movement in the room was restricted. Talking together in the room was considered a violation of the prison regulations. All had to sleep at 9:00 P.M. when the light was put off. This humiliating treatment was a systematic policy. Even in the daily half an hour break, we had to walk in twos, with our heads bent down. One had to say "Master" to the jailer before the jailer would speak to him. Medical care and nutrition situation were no better.

HUNGER STRIKES

In May 1970, we went on a hunger strike. Our demands were: ending the jailers' humiliating treatment; our right to use the blankets and talk together in the rooms; to be allowed to receive fruits from our relatives and the meals to be improved; ending collective punishment and imprisonment in the solitary cells; to have a sponge and soap for bathing; to have beds; to be supplied with a list of rights and liabilities for the prisoners.

In 1973, we went on another strike. We refused to go out during the daily break or meet our relatives during the visits so that they would raise our complaints to the media. We stopped taking baths, shaving or washing our faces and clothes. The prisoners smelt very nasty and the jailers couldn't enter our rooms to give their orders. At last, they met some of our demands such as lifting the metal plates separating the rooms. The daily break became 60 minutes instead of 30 minutes.

In 1975, we had a third strike to put an end to the oppressive and humiliating practices. However, we put our demands into action: No more saying "Master" to the jailer. No more walking in twos with heads bent down during the breaks. We were beaten and put in the solitary cells. But we insisted on the demands and they became our normal actions.

On 11 December 1976, we went on the famous strike that lasted 67 days. Our demands included medical treatment for those who needed it and the right of collective representation.

CONDITIONAL IMPROVEMENT

The prison authorities expressed their "readiness" to improve our conditions if we agreed to work: "Work and your conditions will be improved." We refused the offer on the basis that Geneva Agreement reads that prisoners are allowed to work on condition that the revenue of their work would be returned to them and that the conditions in the places of work should be different from those in the prisoner's rooms. Both conditions were not available to us.

MEDIATION, THREAT, AND DEPORTATION

In spite of the beating and torture, we continued our strike. During that time, Al-Shawwa, Mayor of

Gaza, visited us to mediate an end to the strike. He failed to achieve anything. The next day we were visited by a Knesset member who said: "Your strike is a political one and had nothing to do with living conditions. Outside the prison you threw real bombs. Now you are throwing political bombs inside it."

After that 40 strikers, including myself, were deported to Beit leed prison. On the 45th day of the strike, Haiem Halivi, Director of the prisons, came and promised to meet our demands if we end the strike. We were returned back to Ashkelon prison where we all agreed to end the hunger strike.

FALSE PROMISE

A week later, Halivi came to the prison and looked at us with an openly deceitful and sarcastic smile, as if he had meant to say, "I fooled you." In consequence we decided to resume the hunger strike. The authorities responded by practising the same brutal methods in beating and force-feeding us. They took some of us, including myself, on a "disciplinary mission" to Jalami prison. After 22 days of this new strike, they fulfilled some of our demands. We were supplied with sponge mattresses 5 cms. thick; the daily break became two hours; and we were supplied with the daily English Jerusalem Post.

"C" CATEGORY

The Zionist authorities classify the prisoners in "A", "B" and "C" categories. The first includes the ordinary citizens; the second includes the criminals and those who belong to the underworld in their society; the third includes the Palestinian militants. Jesterfield, the director of the prison, always treated us in this last category. We used to say to him, "Give us the rights your 'state' gives to the criminals of your society." But in his treatment to us, he never tried to deal with us outside his view of us as enemies. He deliberately manifested his hatred towards us.

CONDITIONS FOR DISPLAY ONLY

A visitor to the Ashkelon prison will be fascinated by what he sees and that the situation is supposed to be good. The visitor is shown a basketball court, volley ball court and a tennis table. But to think how about 500 prisoners could possibly practise such sports together in the 30 minutes daily break, makes one realize the truth. The same with the library; it is clean and the books are well arranged. But where are the books to read? In recent years, some political and philosophical books were brought; of course, due to our struggle. The clinic in the prison is not an exception. You can see large quantities of medicine arranged on the shelves. But the medicines given to the patients were only tranquillizers, aspirin, and valium.

KAMAL NAMMARY

Born: 1942 | Arrested: 1968

My political life started when I was a schoolboy in the late 1950s. In 1965, I graduated as a civil engineer from Cairo University and returned to Jordan. In 1966, I was imprisoned by the Jordanian authorities for four months.

After the June War in 1967, our duty was to distribute pamphlets to urge the masses not to leave their houses and land and to confront the occupiers by all means. We succeeded in building a broad political front including all the national forces in the occupied territories. After that, we began the armed resistance against the occupation forces, using whatever light weapons we could secure.

ARREST

Until my arrest on 3 March 1968, I took part in several military operations. Another militant, William Nassar, was also arrested for the same charge.

From the very moment of my arrest, the beating started. I was blindfolded, tied and taken to Sarafand prison. I was punched and kicked in the stomach and everywhere else on my body. They put me in a cell, one meter by one meter in dimension. For four consecutive days, I was prevented from sleep and subjected to beating.

INTERROGATION

I was charged with being a commando leader in the West Bank. They wanted me to give them information about commando bases in Al-Karameh and in the occupied territories. In spite of the brutal torture, I didn't give any information. I was under both physical and psychological torture.

There were two interrogators who adopted different roles, one beating me and the other promising me things if I talked. They threatened to blow up my house if I didn't speak. In fact, they did it. Due to continuous torture, my hand was paralyzed. I began a hunger strike. After seven days, they tried to negotiate with me.

TRIAL

On 6 May, I was taken to court. William was also there. Each session of the trial lasted for five days. We rejected the trial and the lawyer assigned by the court. We refused to stand for the judges as they passed before us. The policemen beat us while we were in the cages. During the trial, we refused to talk as an expression of our non-recognition of the lawfulness of the court.

THREE RELIGIONS

The Zionists used to assume that the Palestinian militants were a "handful of mercenaries and outcasts." The torture we had been under was meant to make us give in and politically breakdown so that they would show us to the world public as such.

Concerning our case, they found themselves with a political problem that refuted all their allegations. I am a civil engineer and William was a university student in Spain. I am a Muslim and he is a Christian. Most critical to them was the fact that both our mothers are Jews. Three religions have been in struggle for the same cause.

NATIONAL UNITY

The enemy didn't differentiate between one militant and another. All were liable to the same oppression and humiliation. So we concluded a framework for national unity. We formed what we called the "Coordination Committee". Every Palestinian organization present at the prison was represented by an equal number of members.

I would proudly say that the militants in the prisons reached a splendid political level. We imposed our respect on our jailers. Now he who would beat a prisoner would be beaten. The prison authorities would manage to transfer him to another place so that we would never see him again.

JEWS, BUT NOT ZIONISTS

Most of the prisoners in Ramle prison were militants of the Palestinian revolution. The others were ordinary civilians. I would classify the Jewish prisoners into two groups. Those who belonged to democratic groups, the best of whom were those who belonged to the Red Front and the others who, to a large extent, belonged to the underworld of the Zionist society.

NAWAF AL-ZARROW

Born: 1950 | Arrested: 1968

After the occupation of the West Bank and Gaza, in June war 1967, it was natural that the people would carry arms and resist occupation. However, within that part of Palestine occupied in 1948, there has been resistance since the Zionists took over, though at a comparatively low level. So to fulfil this duty, some comrades and myself joined the armed struggle in early 1968.

Our first big operation was the "Night of Bombs", on August 18, 1968, in Jerusalem, when 5 explosions occurred at the same time in different districts of the city.

The operation was executed for specific reasons. First it was meant to refute the enemy's allegations that stability had been restored to the city after its so called "re-unification". It was also a response to the enemy's allegations that the Arabs of the city were living in "harmony" with their occupiers, and the whole city was "restored to order." Second, it was meant as a warning against the efforts of the UN emmissary, Gunnar Jarrings, who was then mediating between Israel and the Arab regimes for a solution to the Arab-Israeli conflict, in complete ignorance of the core of the conflict: Palestinian rights.

This operation was followed by the "Night of Horror" operation in Tel-Aviv, on 4 September, after which our group was discovered by the enemy. Except for one comrade and me, all of our group were arrested. We two managed to escape to our hideout. But after an operation against the enemy soldiers in Hebron, our hideout was detected, and we were both arrested when the whole area was filled with soldiers and with helicopters flying above.

ARREST

I say with sorrow that we couldn't resist. Our arms were hidden in another place. Beating and torture started from the moment of our arrest. The soldiers hit us with the butts of their guns, kicked us with their legs and punched us with their fists.

Then we were taken by helicopter to Hebron prison. The interrogation there was supervised by the army's intelligence service, who brought in strong and able-bodied men to interrogate us. Of course, they were well trained for the job with all the experience methods of torture, physical and psychological.

PHYSICAL TORTURE

They cruelly punched our faces and severely hit us on sensitive parts of the body. They kicked our faces with their boots and extinguished cigarettes on our bodies, especially on the nipples and under the arms. We could not move our arms because the burnt skin was irritated and caused pain. Nor could we even sleep. Worse was that they tried to emasculate me.

They hit me very harshly and cruelly on my genitals. This process was repeated several times.

PSYCHOLOGICAL TORTURE

When the physical torture failed to make me give information, they resorted to psychological torture. Once, after being beaten by soldiers and officers, about 20 people surrounded me. Some of them began asking questions in a hurried way leaving me no time for concentration to give an answer, while some others were laughing loudly and hysterically. Still others began loading their weapons and threatened to kill me. This took place in a dark room which helped to create a horrible atmosphere.

Another method of psychological torture was to threaten to detain our relatives, especially our sisters. They threatened to bring my sisters and rape them if I didn't confess. My sisters and young brother were detained in the Maskobeya prison in Jerusalem and were severely tortured.

TRIAL

The trial had seven sessions during which my comrades and myself were brought before the court. The trial was a farcical one. But we changed it into a political forum to express our political opinions. We spoke out strongly about our national cause. The Zionist soldiers, acting on the judges' orders, would beat us and cruelly bring us back to the docks. Our reaction was to sing national songs about Palestine and the revolution. On 9 February 1969, the trial ended with each of us being given a life sentence.

STRUGGLE

In fact, the natural response to hear a life sentence read to you is to be bitterly shocked. But our belief that the Zionist occupation and the Zionist entity itself would not outlive us gave us the strength to begin a new stage of struggle. Our first concern was to keep our morale high and steadfast for the survival of our political identity and revolutionary consciousness. In this context, the struggle inside the prison was considered an extension of the struggle outside.

EDUCATION

The last thing we expect is for our enemy to look after our educational and health needs. The enemy's deliberate policy in prisons is to turn the militants there into reserve manpower for his economy, and to turn them into such a desperate group that those who complete their sentences will leave the prisons with a large gap between them and their community outside. In view of this our concern was to raise our educational and cultural levels to preserve our spirit and political consciousness.

We ran classes for general education and for specific subjects such as history, philosophy, sciences and foreign languages: English, French and Hebrew. Due to our efforts, I can estimate that 90% of our fellow militants who are still in the prison got the G.C.E. level.

GHASSAN KAMAL

Born: 1949 | Arrested: 1968

I was recruited in the Palestinian revolution in 1968. With other militants of my unit, we carried out several successful operations in the Jerusalem and Tel Aviv areas. I was arrested only several minutes after the early explosion of a bomb I had planted, due to a defect in its timing device.

INTERROGATION

The captured evidence made it impossible for me and the other militants to ignore the charges of commitment to the Palestinian revolution. But the interrogators practised all the means of torture against us, so we would give them more details and information. I was hit with fists on the face, stomach and all other parts of the body. Most painful were the kicks on the stomach, the back and the genitals. This lasted for 36 days during which I was under the threat of being shot dead if I did not give the names of other militants or the hiding places of our weapons.

TRIAL

On the day of trial, I was taken with my fellow militants of the same unit to the court. At the beginning we refused to go because the result of the "trial" was already known. They tried to impose their lawyers on us to "defend" us. We refused their lawyers and insisted on defending ourselves. We took the opportunity to defend the cause for which we carried arms and resorted to violence. The court was transferred into a political forum. We exposed the inhuman and brutal treatment we had met during the investigation. The judge ordered the soldiers who were there to shut us up. So, we were violently driven out of the court. Meanwhile, the judge gave us all life sentences.

LIVING CONDITIONS

Contrary to what was expected, beating and inhuman treatment were no less unbearable in the prison. Medical care and food supplies were worse. Humiliation and insults were the daily policy practised by the jailers. So, as freedom fighters who had carried arms to liberate their country and restore their people's dignity, we did not give in, even though we were in prison. We preserved our revolutionary spirit and considered ourselves a relatively active extension of our revolutionary community outside.

MEDICAL CARE

As for the medical treatment, it wasn't an exception to the entire deliberate Zionist policy of destroying us morally and physically. Several wounded militants were left bleeding for a long time or left without medical treatment till their wounds worsened and complications set in.

Hafez Dalkamouni is but one example. His leg could have been saved had he received the correct treatment in time. After being mishandled and neglected for a long time, the "concerned medical authorities" decided his leg should be cut off under the pretext that it was infected with gangrene which would spread. Dalkamouni argued that his injury was slight and he needed treatment not amputation. They said that without amputation they would give him no treatment, so Dalkamouni surrendered to their decision.

CHANGE IN TREATMENT

A remarkable point that is worth mentioning is the change we noticed on the part of some Zionist jailers. Most of the jailers in the Zionist prisons are Oriental Jews. In fact, the director of the prison prevented them from talking with us, except for routine procedural matters. But during the last years of our imprisonment, we were able to hold debates with some of them. To learn Hebrew and other languages was a great benefit to us in this context. We were capable of convincing some of them of the justice of the Palestinian cause. Confronted with our arguments, most of them would say, "You are right. But what can I do? It is not me who makes the decisions."

AIDA SAAD

Born: 1951 | Arrested: 1969

The motive behind my joining the military struggle is the picture which I have grown up with and which still sticks in my memory. It is the picture of the Zionist occupation of the Gaza Strip in 1956. I remember how our young men and children were killed and our houses blown up; how the Israeli jets were bombing and shooting, killing many of us; how the Zionist soldiers were rounding us up in schools and streets. I remember how I was running with my mother, both bare-footed and starving, to escape death. This is the picture that was imprinted in my memory as a child. It made me ask; why are these people killing us?

Early in 1968, I joined the ranks of the Palestinian revolution with full awareness of my choice and destiny. My duty was to take food and weapons to the commandos who were pursued by the enemy, and to convey messages from one base to another.

"I WANT TO RESTORE MY IDENTITY"

On 16 March 1969, I received instructions to go on a splendid mission. In the meantime, I was very emotional. But my love for my people, their pain in the refugee camps, the humiliation of the occupiers erupted in my mind to dominate any other thought and suppress any other consideration.

At midnight, I headed to my target, the Zionist military barrack at Al-Shoja'aya quarter in Gaza. I was determined that the explosion of my grenade would bring down the Zionist entity imposed on my land and make the whole world hear my lesson. I want to restore my homeland... I want to restore my identity. When I drew near the barrack, I felt that I was holding my soul in my hands, and every step forward was drawing me nearer to certain death, but the memory of the bombs and shells thrown on us pushed me to hurry into the barrack. I threw the first grenade... a tank caught fire. I threw the second... another tank caught fire. I was close to the second target so I was struck by some shrapnel. My wounds made it too difficult for me to withdraw in time and avoid the bullets of the guards. Thus I fell captive, and from that moment the beating and torture started.

INTERROGATION, TORTURE

The interrogation started before they gave me any first aid, just after I was arrested. They took off all my clothes under the pretext of checking me. They pulled me by the hair, spat on me, dragged me on the floor, kicked me, and extinguished cigarettes on my body. They wanted to know "the other people" who were with me, and from where I had brought the grenades.

TRIAL

On 14 April 1969, they put me on trial. It was a play more than a trial. I knew that the sentence had already been determined. The moment I got out of the armoured vehicle to enter the court, I saw dozens of my Palestinian people there. I saw the Palestinian children holding bouquets of roses. The smiles of those children, their staring eyes, made it clear to me that they had understood the meaning of what I had done. My mother's looks at that moment were full of love and pride for what I had done. I felt that the bonds between me and my people had become stronger.

Then the trial began. The judge charged me on six counts. The trial was concluded, and I received a 20-year sentence. During the trial, I heard a journalist say, "I want to ask the defendant if she repents what she did." The judge answered, "Her eyes show that she doesn't. Her looks are a sufficient response." I laughed and asked the judge, "How could you know I am not repentant?" At that moment another journalist asked me the same question. "Are you sorry or not?" My answer was that, "Really, I am sorry because I was not able to set off all the grenades that I had."

IN RAMLE PRISON

The prison authorities didn't spare a means to provoke and irritate us. Their aim was to destroy us politically, physically and morally.

PUNITIVE MEASURES

Their treatment to us expressed deliberate hatred. Once, my niece, Suzan, came to visit me with my mother. Before my imprisonment, she loved me very much for my kindness to her. She took a barrette from her hair and gave it to me as an expression of deep affection. The jailer standing beside me prevented me from taking it. I asked her to let me take it and promised to give it to her when my niece left. But she refused. My niece got angry and believed I had refused to take the present. She stopped visiting me until she was 11 years old and understood the situation.

THERESE: A PALESTINIAN ARAB

Therese Halsa was one of my fellow militants in Ramle prison, from Acre city in the 1948 occupied part of Palestine. She was arrested with Rima Tannus after hijacking an airliner to Lydda airport in May 1972. The chauvinist jailers insisted that she speak Hebrew with her mother whenever the latter visited her daughter, under the pretext that Therese was an "Israeli." Therese insisted that she is a Palestinian Arab and that the Arabic language is her mother tongue. Consequently, she refused to meet her mother on that occasion. This case developed to such an extent that the authorities finally gave in.

PALESTINE ON HER HAND

A prison operation on Therese's arm made it almost senseless and resulted in wrinkles on the palm of her hand. Once I saw her sitting looking at her opened hand. "What are you looking at, Therese?" I asked. "Look Aida," she said "now the palm of my hand has turned to a map of Palestine. These wrinkles are the mountains of Jerusalem and Hebron. Here is Acre. This Haifa. This is Jaffa. This Gaza."

RIMA TANNUS

Born: 1952 | Arrested: 1972

I was arrested after my participation in hijacking an airliner from Belgium to Lydda airport in occupied Palestine. The plane had on board some Zionist soldiers who had booked tickets on that airline rather than El Al for security reasons.

I am a Jordanian. The motive behind my joining the Palestinian revolution was the human aspect of the Palestinian cause, not the fact that I am an Arab. The issue of humanity is one; its oneness is universal and cannot be divided.

After the June war, I was deeply impressed by the sight of Palestinian refugees crossing the River Jordan, fleeing the death spread by the Zionist war machine in West Bank and Gaza Strip. I saw how those people were concentrated in camps in tents which could neither protect them against the hot summer nor the cold winter. I began to wonder if I weren't, one day, be transformed into a refugee by the Zionist expansionist policy and face the same conditions.

OPERATION

In spite of the strict security measures in the airport, we succeeded in bringing in with us our weapons and explosives. The plane took off and landed in Vienna before taking off again to Lydda airport. As the plane flew off the Austrian air space, Therese and I rushed to the toilet to get our pistols and explosives ready. Rushing back to the other two militants, Abu Nidal and Zakareya, we gave them the pistols and hurried back to our assigned places in the plane. Abu Nidal then rushed to the cockpit and declared our authority on the plane. He then addressed the passengers, telling them our aim — to offer to release the Zionist soldiers on board in exchange for some of our militants in the Zionist jails.

"WE ARE IN PALESTINE"

Our happiness and pleasure were unimaginable when we entered the Palestinian air space and saw Palestine. We kissed each other, shouting "Now we are in Palestine!" Abu Nidal ordered the captain to land the plane on the airfield in such a way as to hinder the landing and taking off of any other plane.

Negotiations lasted 24 hours with the I.R.C. representative coming and going. The plane ran out of oxygen and the air inside became very stuffy. Humanitarian considerations made Abu Nidal agree that sandwiches be brought to the passengers and fuel to the plane so that the engine would work.

BEATING AND TORTURE

When the shooting was over, the grenade was taken from my hand. My hands and legs were tied by a plastic wire. I was dragged by my hair to the stairs of the plane where I was pushed and rolled down to the ground. Many soldiers were there; some were in vehicles and others were on foot. Several soldiers took turns beating me on the stomach and the head and kicking me on the back. I was then dragged a small distance to where a soldier made me stand up. I found myself facing Moshe Dayan, then Minister of Defence. He asked me my name in Arabic. But when I didn't answer him, he told them to take me away.

INTERROGATION

After that I was taken to another place. The blindfold was taken off my eyes. I found myself seated on a chair in front of some officers wearing their uniform.

They asked me about the organization I belonged to, its leader, the people who cooperated with me in Europe. When they got no answer, they started beating me with sticks on my head and every part of my body.

When they failed to extract any information, they took me to a big room. They took off all my clothes and tied each of my hands and legs to rings fitted in the opposite walls. The interrogation was resumed as I was laid flat on my back. It was interrupted by fierce beating and extinguishing cigarettes on my body. Cold and hot water was also poured on me.

IN RAMLE PRISON

Rather than the beating and torture I had been suffering, I was always worrying about Therese. I knew that there were other militants in the prison who would hear my crying when I was under torture. They delivered to me their encouragement to keep my morale high and not to break down.

TRIAL

One day in August 1972, we were taken to the court. Our trial lasted about two weeks. We asked that Valencia Langer defend us, but they refused. They assigned us a lawyer of their own. The charges against me were many: carrying arms, commitment to an "illegal" organisation, hijacking a plane, deliberate killing. The trial was concluded and both of us, Therese and I, received life sentences.

LIVING CONDITIONS

Living conditions are very bad. Food is insufficient, whether one is speaking of quantity or quality. Medical care was very bad. We used to go on hunger strikes demanding an improvement in the medical care. Our strikes were brutally suppressed.

EDUCATION

From 2-5 P.M., our time was free. After lunch we would use some time to educate ourselves. The I.R.C. supplied us with books and stationery for that purpose. We were taught Arabic, English, French, and Hebrew. We had some non-Arab political prisoners who helped in the teaching process, including Terre Fleener, an American from Texas, Brigit, a German, and Ludvina, a Dutch.

RASMEYA AUDI

Born: 1948 | Arrested: 1969

At midnight on 28 February 1969, my family and I were awakened by repeated strong knocks on the door. As soon as my father opened it, we saw him pushed back by the Zionist soldiers thrusting the barrels of their rifles against his chest. At that moment, some of them started beating us while others began searching the house after turning everything upside down. Then we were blindfolded and our hands tied. The soldiers took us all, my parents, my paralyzed sister, and myself, to the Maskobeya (Russian Compound) prison in Jerusalem. This was after my participation in two military operations in Jerusalem.

In Maskobeya prison they separated me from the others. Several interrogators surrounded me and started beating me. Meanwhile they were laughing hysterically to make me break down. One of them was beating me on my head with an iron rod.

They brought my parents and sisters, even Fatima the paralyzed one, before me and started beating them. They said I had to choose between confession of the charges made against me or my family would continue to be tortured and our house blown up. Unable to bear the screaming of my parents, and especially of my dear sister, poor Fatima, I confessed to all the charges they made. Nevertheless, our house was blown up and the torture continued.

TORTURE

During the interrogation I suffered three kinds of torture: physical, psychological and sexual. Due to the blows against my head, I lost hearing in one of my ears for about a year. Many times I was completely stripped and thrown on the floor. Rather than beat and kick me, they would extinguish cigarettes all over my body. I was pinched in various places, mainly my breasts, causing my body to turn black and blue.

They brought my father, an old man in poor health, and started beating me before him till my mouth began bleeding. My father rushed to me and took me in his arms. Then they violently separated us, and forcefully took my clothes off. They ordered him to take off all his clothes and have sex with me. Upon his refusal, they started beating him and taking off his clothes. As soon as they took off his jacket, he lost consciousness and broke down.

NOT TO BE PASSED BY

Sexual torture against women is a deliberate Israeli policy. From the very beginning of our revolution, our enemy realized the risks posed by the participation of Arab women, in general, and Palestinian women in particular in the struggle. They realized how sensitive this matter is to Arabs. They believed that such torture would make traditional parents think many times before they let their daughters take part in the struggle, due to certain considerations of honour which women stand for in a traditional family.

IN RAMLE PRISON

After the trial, I was taken with ten others to the Ramle (Women's) prison. There we met the fellow militants. In our first days there we were faced with cruel treatment. The prison authorities used some Israeli women prisoners to torture and trouble us. They mobilized them against us by telling them that we were "criminals and murderers" and pushed them into beating us.

HUNGER STRIKE

The weekly visit allowed to our relatives was turned into a monthly one. Bringing books to the prison, even at our relatives' expense, was forbidden. The only way we could change the situation was to declare a hunger strike.

The hunger strike lasted for 12 consecutive days, after which the prison authorities complied with our demands and brought us books. They also made some changes in the visiting procedure. Monthly visits were allowed for 3 adult relatives or two adults and two youngsters.

Our strike was successful due to our unified stand against the prison authorities. This unified stand was intensified by the fact that the authorities did not, and do not, distinguish between prisoners from the different Palestinian organizations. We were all subjected to the same torture and insults. We achieved national unity from our first days in prison. The spirit of democracy prevailed among us. We would argue and debate all subjects in an open, democratic way.

ALIA ABU DAYYA

Born: (Information withheld) | Arrested: (Information withheld)

The testimony of Alia Abu Dayya, the final witness in this collection, continues the documentation of Palestinian political prisoners' experiences in Israeli jails. Her account details conditions in Ramle Women's Prison, the psychological and physical methods employed against female detainees, and the sustained efforts to maintain dignity and revolutionary spirit in the face of systematic oppression.

Like those who came before her, Alia's testimony speaks to the collective will of Palestinian prisoners who refused to allow their captivity to sever them from their cause, their people, or their identity.

WORLD: MILITANTS

The following section documents the broader international context of political imprisonment and solidarity — recognizing that the Palestinian struggle against occupation and for prisoner rights did not exist in isolation, but as part of a global movement of peoples resisting oppression.

Palestinian prisoners, throughout their years of confinement, maintained awareness of and solidarity with liberation movements around the world. Their study circles followed international developments; their political education incorporated the struggles of peoples from Vietnam to South Africa. This international consciousness strengthened their resolve and gave them a sense of belonging to a larger human community of resistance.

The liberation of 76 Palestinian political prisoners on 14 March 1979 was not simply a prisoner exchange — it was a statement about the power of steadfastness, the legitimacy of resistance, and the ultimate failure of oppression to extinguish the human will to be free.

— End —

www.ingramcontent.com/pod-product-compliance
Lightning Source LLC
Jackson TN
JSHW070023160726
105219JS00005B/259
* 9 7 9 8 3 3 0 5 3 2 0 2 5 *